I love a book that [illegible] ys seems to drive me t[illegible] *m-en in The Bible* ac[illegible] to women are simple, [illegible] meet with Christ at the throne of grace.

Chrissy Toledo
Author, Girl In The Song

As a wife, mom, leader, friend, we are constantly seeking wisdom on how to live out God's purpose amidst the noise of life. Brenda's book, *The Deeper Life of Women in the Bible,* not only unwraps the strength, vulnerability, and faithfulness of the women of the Bible but gives us practical ways to incorporate these spiritual principles into our own life. This book is a perfect combination of teaching and inspiration that leaves you with a clearer vision of how to live life on purpose.

Dana Spinola
Founder & CEO of fab'rik
Author, Love What you Do

Brenda has combined my two greatest loves into one dynamic Bible study: God's Word and the stories of real women who struggle and discover the deeper attributes of God. If you have felt stuck or lethargic in your walk with God, this Bible study will revive your love for God and His living, active Word. Grab some girlfriends or find some younger women to mentor during this season of your life and walk together through *The Deeper Life of Women in the Bible.*

Linda Barrick
Founder of Hope Out Loud
Author, Beauty Marks & Miracle for Jen

Our friendship began in a remote and dusty village of Guatemala, where I saw firsthand Brenda's deep love for God and compassion for the world. She has truly discovered the "deeper life" for herself and I can't think of a better guide to lead us through these truths our souls long to know and understand.

Noel Yeatts
President, World Help
Author, Awake, Doing a World of Good One Person at a Time

Brenda has written an excellent and thought-provoking book examining the deeper life. She draws from eight women in the Bible and takes us on an exciting journey to examine our theology, our security in Christ and our personal priorities in life. As you read her clear and insightful wisdom, you will be challenged and encouraged to desire a closer, more intimate relationship with our Lord. She asks insightful questions and gives practical assignments that are beneficial for personal growth or group Bible study discussions. She has skillfully woven a biblical tapestry of cultures and customs that remain timeless and relevant to our everyday spiritual lives.

Alice Moss
Strategic Renewal Board Member
Author, I Crossed Over

THE DEEPER LIFE

of Women in the Bible

Eight Enduring Women who Discovered a Deeper Life

BRENDA BROWN

STRATEGIC RENEWAL

Published by Strategic Renewal
www.strategicrenewal.com
Printed in the United States of America

ISBN 978-1-7341973-2-7
Emphasis in Scripture shown by italics is the author's.

Contents

Foreword 7

Introduction: Where are You? 9

1. **A Deeper Look at Hagar** 13
   The Question: Who is God?
   The Issue: My theology

2. **A Deeper Look at Ruth** 21
   The Question: Who am I?
   The Issue: My identity

3. **A Deeper Look at Esther** 27
   The Question: Why am I here?
   The Issue: My purpose

4. **A Deeper Look at the Daughters of Zelophehad** 33
   The Question: What really matters?
   The Issue: My values

5. **A Deeper Look at Priscilla** 39
   The Question: What shall I do?
   The Issue: My priorities

6. **A Deeper Look at Lydia** 45
   The Question: How shall I do it?
   The Issue: My goals

7. **A Deeper Look at the Samaritan Woman** 51
   The Question: When shall I do it?
   The Issue: My time

8. **A Deeper Look at Eunice** 57
   The Question: How will I finish?
   The Issue: My legacy

Epilogue – One Last Stop 63

Foreword

As a young woman in my teens I had a fascination with the lives of the women in the Bible. I read biblical commentaries about them, did Bible studies about them and devoured historical fiction about many of these women. Currently, I am reading another historical novel about Hannah. Sarah was always a favorite for me because the biblical account of her life seemed to resonate with my heart as I pursued my faith and learned to trust God. A theme that has carried over into my adult life as I have followed and pursued obedience to the Lord in a life filled with uncertainties and unknowns. I believed, and still do, that these women were important to God and their accounts were placed in Scripture so that I could learn from them. They each had a purpose to fulfill and an assured destiny.

As women, we are daughters, sisters, wives, mothers, aunts, grandmothers, girlfriends, leaders and influencers and God has uniquely created each of us and placed within us a deep longing to know Him and to fulfill the purpose for which we are created. In the "dailiness" of life it is so easy to lose sight of that priority. But often it is even harder to know what fulfilling God's purposes should look like for me individually if I don't have a foundation or understanding of how to define those priorities and live them out each day.

Brenda Brown has beautifully melded the accounts of some interesting women in the Scriptures along with the most important questions you will ever answer. Brenda has answered these questions in her own life and has a deep desire to help other women look honestly at these questions in order to experience greater fulfillment and satisfaction. As you engage in this study and answer these questions for you personally, you will have the tools to not only verbalize, but live out, God's purpose in a way that will help you see yourself with a fresh perspective and be empowered to live your life with more intention. Just as the women in the Bible have left a legacy for us, we will also leave a legacy one day -- and may it be one of authenticity and significance in light of eternity. But in order to do that we must first start at the beginning with the most important question.

Blessings to you as you embark on this journey of faith and pursue a greater understanding of what really matters in this life. I am confident that you will experience a deeper, more purposeful life and bring great glory to our God!

Rosemary Henderson
Strategic Renewal International

Introduction

For everything that was written in the past was written to teach us, so that through the endurance taught in the Scriptures and the encouragement they provide we might have hope.

Romans 15:4

As I write this, our world is in the throes of the COVID-19 outbreak. Social-distancing and self-quarantining are the buzz words of the day. No one knows what the future holds. Coronavirus has spread across the planet, infecting millions and killing hundreds of thousands. The global economy has suffered, and jobless claims continue to rise. Two months ago, I had a calendar filled with a busy schedule of meetings, luncheons and travel. Today, I am secluded in my home, away from friends, family, and fellowship. How quickly life as we know it has halted.

Social media is full of reasons and remedies for our current pandemic. There are some who promise that this season will be short, while others warn that it will be long. The truth is that no one knows. Our future is unknown. Like so many generations before us, we are suddenly reminded that much – so much – is out of our control. Stripped of all the superficial trappings of life, we are left with our thoughts and looking for answers.

Thankfully, we don't have to look far. We have the stories of biblical heroines to inspire us. Women who were stripped of everything. Women who stepped out and stepped up. Women who bravely pioneered the path to a deeper life and left footprints that we can follow. Let's travel together through the pages of Scripture and drop in on a few of my favorite women. Along the way, we'll discover their secret for living a deeper life.

Let's Begin Where we all Began

DNA testing and lineage tracing have become very popular in recent years. It's fascinating to discover distant cousins and read stories of the hardships of our ancestors. Their stories become personal as soon as their branch gets added to the family tree. Have you ever considered that if you could trace your family line back to the beginning, it would eventually list Eve as your 100th (or so) great-grandmother?[1] Suddenly her story becomes personal. It is part of your family tree. If it's been awhile since you've read it, open up your family album and picture Grandma Eve in Genesis chapter 3.

Where are you?

As a grandmother of preschoolers, I get to play hide-and-seek quite a bit. Before the counting even begins, I know where the little ones are going to hide. As soon as the announcement of "ready or not, here I come" is made, I hear the giggles and squeals.

Why is this game so much fun for children? Could it be that deep down we all like to be pursued? Sought out?

In Genesis 3, no one was giggling during the original game of hide-and-seek. After disobeying God's specific instruction in the Garden of Eden, Adam and Eve hid. God then pursued, calling out to the couple, "Where are you?" Did the Lord know where they were? Of course. And yet, He asked the question that He needed them to answer.

As we begin this journey, we must start with this simple question – "Where are you?" The wonderful thing about God is that He already knows where you are. Imagine Him walking into the room and calling your name. If He were to take a seat across from you and ask, *where are you right now? What are your dreams? In what areas are you struggling?* How would you answer Him? Whatever your answer, He will meet you where you are, and then show you what to do next.

---

1 https://answersingenesis.org/bible-timeline/genealogy/how-many-human-generations-are-there-from-adam-until-today/

What if your answer is a bit messy? Perhaps your day started with good intentions, but one slip up led to another. Pretty soon your footing gave way altogether and the tumble downward began. Maybe you are ashamed of your behavior and dreading how God will respond. We well remember the consequences of Eve's actions – especially the "pain in childbearing" part. But do you remember what else happened on that fateful day? Read Genesis 3:21.

God confronted Eve's sin, but then He clothed her with garments of skin. Our 100th great-grandmother Eve was God's first daughter. He provided for her needs and He ordained His daughter with a high and holy calling – to be mother of all the living. Eve's life was spared because God still had a great purpose in mind for her.

So, where are you? The game is up. No more hiding or pretending to be something you're not. God already knows where you are and how you got there. He's counted to 10 and announced, "Ready or not, here I come!" Your Father is in pursuit of you. I hope you're squealing with delight!

One Step at a Time

As we begin this journey to a deeper life, we'll need to lay a firm foundation as we clarify our theology. We'll then discover that our theology is the basis of our identity. Our identity shapes our purpose. Our purpose guides our values. Our values determine our priorities. Our priorities are implemented by our goals. Our goals are accomplished by our stewardship of time. All of this, when understood clearly and embraced daily, results in a legacy that really matters.

Each chapter of this study will focus on one enduring woman who found the answer to an important question we each must ask ourselves. Discovery exercises are included at the end of each chapter to help you address these questions and develop Deeper Life Summary Statements. Once your Deeper Life Statements are clarified, record them in back of the book, beginning on page 70.

Group Discussion Questions

1. How often do you start your morning with good intentions, but feel defeated by day's end?
2. Where are you right now? Describe your season of life.
3. Look over the 8 questions in the Table of Contents. Which question do you most want answered with this study?

A Deeper Look at Hagar

Who is God?

My Theology

Have you ever considered that all of your life is ultimately
an expression of your theology?

-- Daniel Henderson

First steps are always exciting! Are you ready to begin? We've established our starting point by answering the question, "where are you?" It is now time to set out. Today our path leads through the desert. The trail is hot and dusty – maybe not the trip you anticipated. If you're looking around for a shortcut, you might miss out on a great adventure. So, keep walking. We're about to lay the foundation by answering the question, "Who is God?"

Please read Genesis chapter 16

As Sarai's slave, Hagar was given to Abram for the purpose of conceiving a son. Her pregnancy, however, produced a few unintended consequences. Hagar despised Sarai and Sarai mistreated Hagar. Hagar eventually fled. But God pursued. When the Angel of the Lord found Hagar in the desert in Genesis 16:8, what question did he ask her?

Coming upon Hagar at the spring by the road to Shur, the angel specifically addressed the young Egyptian woman by name. The Angel of the Lord is often identified in the Old Testament as the Preincarnate Christ. Whether it was Christ Himself or a heavenly messenger sent on the Lord's behalf, this was not a chance encounter. Hagar was about to become the mother of innumerable descendants. But first she needed to answer a couple of questions — *where have you come from* and *where are you going?* After answering honestly, Hagar is then told by the angel to return to her mistress. She is even told to name her son, Ishmael, which means "God hears."

An encounter with God can change everything. After her heavenly encounter, what name did Hagar give to the Lord? (Genesis 16:13)

___

Ultimately, what you think about when the word "God" comes to mind is the most important thing about you. Your identity, purpose, values, priorities, goals and the way you use your time will all stand or fall on this foundation.

A Deeper Foundation

Several years ago, we had a decision to make. We were given two quotes for a new brick patio on the back of our house. One quote was significantly higher than the other. It was given to us by a friend and well-respected contractor in the area. The cheaper quote was from the contractor our neighbors used for their brick patio. But our friend's words stuck in our minds – "You'll remember the quality long after you've forgotten the price." We trusted him and went with his company. As the work began and their equipment tore up our yard, I wondered if it was all worth it. I didn't remember our neighbor's yard being torn up this much. Their patio only took a couple of days to install. Ours took a couple of weeks. Keeping two children in the house and away from the mess also proved to be a challenge that I didn't anticipate. At the end of the project, our patio looked similar to our neighbor's, but at a much higher price. It wasn't until two years later that the differences became apparent. Our neighbor's patio began to buckle. Weeds had sprouted between their brick pavers. Our patio still looked new. The difference? The deeper foundation of our patio and the attention to time-consuming details of thorough work. Our friend was right. The quality of the final product was well worth the investment.

In order to build a solid foundation, we must first clear out any obstacles that are hindering our understanding of God. The first stumbling block is presuppositions from the home in which we grew up. Even those who grew up in a Christian home are not immune from inaccurate and distorted ideas about God. Next, we need to weed-out our own conjured up views of God that are not rooted in biblical truth.

Paul exhorts us to grow in our knowledge of Christ so that "we will no longer be immature like children. We won't be tossed and blown about by every wind of new teaching. We will not be influenced when people try to trick us with lies so clever they sound like the truth." (Ephesians 4:14 NLT) Reflect on the following questions, and then answer honestly:

1. What are some obstacles that have hindered my view of God?

2. What am I doing to combat those obstacles so that I can gain a clear understanding of God?

For the Christian, a relationship with the Living God begins with the realization that *yes, there is a God and it's not that I must find Him – He's already found me!* Although He is sovereign, great, holy and powerful, God is full of grace and sent His Son, Jesus, to reconcile us to Himself. He is the God who is actively involved in my life and is shaping my future into a plan that has significance. In short, He sees me and He hears me.

Developing a Personal Theology Statement

So how do we take the ocean of biblical truth about God and distill it down to our thimble of understanding? Among all the attributes and names of God, which should you focus on for the sake of daily renewal? The following exercises will help you write out your personal theology statement in answer to the question "Who is God?"

Theology Discovery: My Struggles – His Character

Review the list of common personal struggles. Rank each one from 1 to 5, with 1 being never and 5 being frequent.

____ Addictions
____ Anxiety
____ Anger
____ Apathy
____ Bitterness
____ Broken relationships
____ Controlling
____ Coveting
____ Craving comfort
____ Critical
____ Depression
____ Dishonesty
____ Discontent
____ Discouragement
____ Doubt
____ Fear
____ Gluttony
____ Greed
____ Insecurity
____ Isolation
____ Laziness
____ Loneliness
____ Lust/sensuality
____ Materialism
____ Moodiness
____ Negativity
____ Pride
____ Selfishness
____ Self-doubt
____ Self-promotion
____ Starved for attention
____ Uncertainty
____ Unkindness
____ Unloving

Now, identify four or five of those that ranked the highest. Using the list below, select one of the attributes of God associated with that struggle that you feel would best spark daily renewal. This will allow you to experience a daily renewal in the truth of God's character in order to overcome common personal struggles.

Addictions — Omnipotent, Gracious, Holy
Anxiety — Sovereign, Omniscient, Wise, Good
Anger — Long-Suffering, Sovereign, Merciful, Forgiving
Apathy — Holy, Faithful, Long-Suffering, Loving

Bitterness — Forgiving, Gracious, Merciful, Kind, Long-suffering
Broken relationships — Forgiving, Gracious, Merciful, Long-Suffering
Controlling — Sovereign, Trustworthy, Peace
Coveting — All-sufficient, Good, Just, Provider
Craving comfort — Good, Omniscient, Portion
Critical — Gracious, Forgiving, Merciful, Loving
Depression — Joy, All-Sufficient, Faithful
Dishonesty — Truth, Immutable, Holy, Righteous
Discontent — Good, All-sufficient, Wise
Discouragement — Faithful, Omniscient, Incomprehensible, Good
Doubt — Truth, Omniscient, Immutable, Wise
Fear — Sovereign, Good, Omniscient, Omnipotent, Omnipresent
Gluttony — Self-control, Omnipotent
Greed — Sovereign, Good, Righteous
Insecurity — Good, Faithful, Loving, Omnipotent
Isolation — Sovereign, Omnipresent, Triune
Laziness — Omniscient, Omnipotent
Loneliness — Omnipresent, Loving, Faithful
Lust/sensuality — Holy, Omniscient, Righteous, Omnipotent
Materialism — Eternal, Good, Faithful
Moodiness — Good, Long-Suffering, Immutable
Negativity — Good, Immutable, Sovereign
Pride — Sovereign, Holy, Omnipotent, Infinite
Selfishness — Righteous, Loving, Gracious, Merciful
Self-doubt — Truthful, Wise, Omnipotent
Self-promotion — Holy, Sovereign
Starved for attention — Omnipresent, Omniscient, Loving
Stressed/overwhelmed — Gracious, Just, Long-Suffering, Omnipotent, Omnipresent
Uncertainty — Sovereign, Righteous, Good, Omniscient, Immutable, Incomprehensible
Unkindness — Long-Suffering, Merciful, Gracious, Loving, Good
Unloving — Loving, Long-Suffering, Gracious, Good

Applying My Personal Theology

Reflecting on your answers, select the names or attributes of God that seem especially relevant to your unique challenges and individual journey. Use the following page to describe the difference this will make in your daily life as you begin to craft a personal Theology Statement.

Example:

My God is ***Sovereign***
Therefore ***I do not have to be anxious because I know He is in control and has a perfect plan for my life.***

My God is . . .

Therefore . . .

My God is . . .

Therefore . . .

My God is . . .

Therefore . . .

My God is . . .

Therefore . . .

Once this exercise is completed, you can record it in the Deeper Life Summary at the back of the book.

Go deeper by reflecting on your Great Moments with God and other Theology Discovery exercises in *The Deeper Life* book.

Group Discussion Questions

1. Reflect on the name that Hagar gave to the Lord in Genesis 16:13. How might that encounter have impacted her?
2. Describe a memorable experience when you were aware of God's presence. How did it influence your view of God?
3. Share one struggle you face and the applicable attribute of God that will help you confront that struggle.

A Deeper Look at Ruth

Who Am I?

My Identity

A healthy self-image is seeing yourself as God sees you. No more. No less.
— *Daniel Henderson*

After answering the first question, "Who is God," we can now take the next step on our journey as we consider the basis of our identity and answer the question, "Who am I?"

Deep Roots

Several years ago we toured New Orleans' City Park. As the guide described the devastation to the park from Hurricane Katrina, he said something very interesting. The park is home to the largest collection of mature live oak trees in the world, with the oldest trees between 600 and 800 years old. These massive trees survived the winds and flood that destroyed so much of that city. While the park lost about 1,000 trees, 13,000 others survived. The secret? Their deep roots.

As we seek to become a woman of endurance, we must be rooted in the knowledge of God. Our theology then shapes our identity and gives us the ability to weather the storms of life.

Our Struggle with Identity

Do you know who you are? Many of us are still trying to figure that out. Others have chosen a certain identity and have invested a great deal of time establishing it before a watching world. Some women provide enough status updates, pins and tweets to completely remove all mystery about who they are or how they spend their days. The flawless photos of happy families posted on Facebook and Instagram create images that occasionally mask the very real internal battles with which many women struggle. A truly healthy view of self amounts to seeing yourself as God sees you. No more. No less.

Please read Ruth, chapter 1

Ruth was a woman ripe for a full blown identity crisis. Although born and raised in Moab, Ruth became acquainted with a man named Mahlon. He was the new guy in town, a stranger from Bethlehem with peculiar religious beliefs and customs. She eventually married Mahlon and moved in with his family, accepting the new religion of the Ephrathite boys and their mother. However, before any children were born to the newlyweds, tragedy struck the family. Mahlon and his brother both died, leaving Ruth, her mother-in-law Naomi, and sister-in-law, Orpah, alone and destitute.

Rather than give in to self-pity, Ruth picked herself up by her sandal-straps and began a journey of discovery, beginning with choosing her God. She traveled with Naomi to the strange land of Bethlehem and prepared herself to face some very difficult circumstances. It must have been a humbling excursion for the women. As they walked the rugged route over a period of several days, there would be no tweets, glamorous Instagram pictures or self-promoting posts to help create an image of two eligible women looking for adventure. They were simply a couple of poor widows returning home with empty arms and broken hearts. And yet, Ruth persevered. Read Ruth 2:1-5.

1. What was the name of the relative living in Bethlehem?

   ____

2. What was Boaz's question in verse 5?

   ____

Upon seeing Ruth, Boaz asked his foreman, "Who is that young woman over there?" (NLT) The answer to that question eventually led to a wedding for the couple. Now read Ruth 4:13-17. The baby born to Ruth and Boaz was named ______________________. He became the father of ______________________ who then became the father of ____________________________.

In chapter one of this book, Ruth had a choice. She could have chosen, like her sister-in-law, to return to her "old" identity as a Moabite and worshiper of the god Chemosh. But Ruth made the better choice. She chose to embrace her new identity, which began with a God who created her and by His grace, called her to be His. The result? Read Matthew 1:5. This amazing woman, great-grandmother of King David, is named in the lineage of Christ. Wow - talk about an identity transformation!

As women, it is imperative that we understand our identity. Our identity influences those around us and impacts generations that will come after us. In light of your life's journey, review the truths of what God says to be true about you. Circle those that best articulate what you need for daily reminders of your identity.

I AM ACCEPTED IN CHRIST

John 1:2	I am God's child
John 15:15	I am Christ's friend
Romans 5:1	I have been justified
1 Cor. 6:17	I am united with the Lord and one with Him in spirit
1 Cor. 6:20	I have been bought with a price; I belong to God
1 Cor. 12:27	I am a member of Christ's Body
Ephesians 1:1	I am a saint
Ephesians 1:5	I have been adopted as God's child
Ephesians 2:18	I have direct access to God through the Holy Spirit

Colossians 1:14	I have been redeemed and forgiven of all my sins
Colossians 2:10	I am complete in Christ

I AM SECURE IN CHRIST

Romans 8:1, 2	I am free forever from condemnation
Romans 8:28	I am assured that all things work together for good
Romans 8:33, 34	I am free from any condemning charges against me
Romans 8:35	I cannot be separated from the love of God
2 Cor. 1:21	I have been established, anointed, and sealed by God
Colossians 3:3	I am hidden with Christ in God
Philippians 1:6	I am sure that the good work God has begun in me will be perfected
Philippians 3:20	I am a citizen of heaven
2 Timothy 1:7	I have been given a spirit of power, love and a sound mind
Hebrews 4:16	I can find grace and mercy in time of need
1 John 5:18	I am born of God and the evil one cannot touch me

I AM SIGNIFICANT IN CHRIST

Matthew 5:13, 14	I am the salt and light of the earth
John 15:15	I am a branch of the true vine, a channel of His life
John 15:16	I have been chosen and appointed to bear fruit
Acts 1:8	I am a personal witness of Christ
1 Cor. 3:16	I am God's temple

2 Cor. 5:17-20	I am a minister of reconciliation
2 Cor. 6:1	I am God's co-worker
Ephesians 2:6	I am seated with Christ in the heavenly realm
Ephesians 2:10	I am God's workmanship
Ephesians 3:12	I may approach God with freedom and confidence
Philippians 4:13	I can do all things through Christ who strengthens me

(Taken from "Living Free in Christ" by Neil Anderson 1993, Regal Books)

With these key truths in mind, now make an attempt to write a basic statement about your essential identity including any applications you feel are helpful. Don't worry about perfecting this statement; just let this be a starting point.

____

____

____

____

Example:

I, Brenda Brown, am a beloved daughter of the Sovereign Lord. I am embraced by my Father's love and esteemed by His indwelling Spirit for the purpose of encouraging others to experience His eternal love.

Once this exercise is completed, you can record it in the Deeper Life Summary at the back of the book.

Go deeper by learning about your S-DNA and completing additional Identity Discovery exercises in *The Deeper Life* book.

Group Discussion Questions

1. How do you think social media has affected the expression of our identities?
2. How did Ruth's experiences shape her identity?
3. With spiritual birth comes the understanding of our true identity. If you have been born again[2], describe how that experience has changed your identity.

2 John 3:3. To be born again (or born from above), is an act of God imparting eternal life into a believer. To receive eternal life, you must repent of sin (tell God you're sorry) and receive Jesus Christ as your Lord and Savior. See Appendix 1

A Deeper Look at Esther

Why am I Here?

My Purpose

Until a person knows why he or she is here, that person's life really has no meaning.

— *Daniel Henderson*

We are making progress! Hopefully you've removed some hindrances and lightened your load as you continue this journey. The joy of knowing your God and understanding who you are may have put a little spring in your step.

Today we're going to stroll through the corridors of a palace. Have you ever toured a castle? Everything is shiny and clean and orderly. Royal servants are available to attend to every need. Sounds perfect - unless you're in my tour group, in which case you might want to slip on some running shoes.

A Royal Race

Serving as a chaperone for a high school trip to London, I was thoroughly enjoying my first visit to England. Touring Kensington Palace held the potential for another special memory with my group of students. As we stood outside, I chatted with the girls around me about castles, princesses, and living happily ever after. After waiting in the long line of tourists, we finally entered the palace. It was breathtaking. Unfortunately, while I was admiring the opulence of the royal furnishings, I didn't immediately notice the departure of one of my assigned students. As soon as I realized he was gone, I flew through the palace, calling his name and pushing my way between the throng of people. Suddenly the fun of the afternoon was forgotten. The primary purpose of chaperoning is to guard those in your care. Nothing else mattered in that moment. I finally caught up with the lost student in the last room of the tour. As a young man with Asperger's Syndrome, he had become overwhelmed with the crowd of people and simply headed for the exit. The relief of finding him safe provided a very happy ending and an important reminder of the purpose of my assignment.

A Royal Assignment

Queen Esther's story is one of my favorites. It has palace intrigue, a beautiful heroine, and of course, a happy ending.

Esther discovered the answer to the question, "Why am I here?" Her journey to becoming queen and understanding her purpose began with two foundational questions – "Who is God?" and "Who am I?" By answering these two questions, Esther was eventually able to embrace her purpose and fulfill God's unique plan for her life. It's a short book and worth reading all 10 chapters.

Growing up as a Jewish girl in the home of her cousin, Mordecai, young Esther (also called Hadassah) would have been taught about God on a daily basis. She was confident of her theology. But, as Esther grew and began to understand her identity, things got a little complicated.

Read Esther 2:1-10. Why did she keep her identity a secret?

____

For a time, Esther's secret benefited her. Esther 2:15-18 describes Esther's meeting with the king. What was the result of this divine appointment?

____

____

Wow. Little orphaned Esther grew into a beautiful woman who became queen. It's the fairytale dream of every little girl. A world of potential opened up for Esther as soon as King Xerxes[3] placed the crown on her royal head. Before we assume the words "happily ever after" will come next, we need to keep reading. This story also had a villain. His name was Haman. Chapter three describes how Haman convinced the king to destroy every Jew throughout the entire empire. Now read Esther 4:1-3. How did the people react to this decree?

Suddenly Esther's identity would become critical and her purpose evident. Read Esther 4:13-17.

Esther faced potential death by approaching the king. However, her purpose was clear. Her people were about to be destroyed. She could no longer hide her identity. In the space below, write out her purpose based on Esther 4:14:

The remainder of the book describes the incredible drama and intrigue as the villain gets discovered, Mordecai becomes honored, and the Jewish people are spared. All because Queen Esther embraced her identity and fulfilled her purpose.

Before we say good-bye to Esther, please take a moment to read one more passage in Esther 9:20-28.

If you're like me, you love happy endings. Could Esther ever have imagined such an outcome? The nation of Israel still celebrates Purim today. Schools and businesses close for the day, children dress up in costume and celebrations include parades in the streets. Each year, baskets of food are delivered to neighbors and the story of Esther is read in its entirety with much audience participation. The legacy of a simple woman who knew her God, embraced her identity and fulfilled her purpose has been honored throughout the

3 Some translations use the name, Ahsuerus, the Hebrew transliteration of the Persian name, Khshayarsha.

generations. God accomplished all He had intended in Esther's life. Trust Him to do the same in yours.

Discovering Your Purpose

A wise man once said, "Great minds have purposes. Others have wishes." Are you spending your life wishing and wondering, or do you have a God-given purpose that compels you? Once you are able to capture the vital essence of your *eternal, earthly*, and *explicit* purposes, you will no longer be discouraged with days that feel meaningless.

Your Eternal Purpose:

The Westminster Catechism states that *The chief end of man is to glorify God, and enjoy Him forever.* This reflects the purpose behind our very existence now and in eternity. In the space below, write out your own statement about God's eternal purpose for your life. (It may be the same as the Westminster statement or slightly modified to reflect your unique thoughts):

Your Earthly Purpose:

What thoughts do you have about your unique purpose on this earth, as a specific expression of your theology and identity? Can you specifically and passionately articulate your mission on earth? Consider what you would like to be chiseled on your tombstone and write a summary paragraph:

Your Explicit Purposes:

Explicit purpose statements help us to clarify the purpose of our daily roles and relationships. Use the following chart to list some of the various roles in your life. Next to each role, write a brief statement that describes your explicit purpose in that role *during this season of your life.*

Role	Purpose
Mother	My purpose as a mother to my adult children is to be their ally - by supporting and honoring their marriages and families and making every effort to be an encouragement to them. To give advice and counsel . . . *when asked.*
Role	**Purpose**

Role	Purpose
Role	**Purpose**

Once this exercise is completed, you can record it in the Deeper Life Summary at the back of the book.

Go deeper by studying Christ's earthly purpose and completing additional Purpose Discovery exercises in *The Deeper Life* book.

Group Discussion Questions

1. Purpose instills within us the power of determination. How did Mordecai's words help Esther discover her purpose? (Esther 4:14-16)

2. Describe what you believe to be your earthly purpose. If a holiday were declared in your honor, how would you want to be remembered?

3. Share with the group one of your explicit purposes for this season. Explain the role or relationship and your Explicit Purpose Statement for that role.

A Deeper Look at the Daughters of Zelophehad

What Really Matters?

My Values

Life . . . is a contest that requires clarity and conviction about the principles that make for satisfaction and significance.

— *Daniel Henderson*

We ended our study of Queen Esther with a happy ending. There is much satisfaction in a good outcome. Be assured that you have a good outcome waiting for you at the end of this journey. Today we'll eavesdrop on an inquiry about rules and hold our breath as we await the outcome of that conversation.

Playing by the Rules

During the recent COVID-19 "shelter-in-place" order, many of us have dusted off long forgotten board games in an effort to recapture family game night. It reminds me of a friend's experience with playing the game "Sorry!" with her young children. Assuming that the rules were easy enough for both girls to follow, the parents set up the "Sorry!" board with great anticipation for a fun evening. If you've ever played this game with young children, then you might know what happened next. As the game progressed, tensions grew. Camaraderie was exchanged for competitiveness. Squabbling quickly turned to sobbing. The game was eventually packed up, put away and banished from family night.

I well remember being sorry for bringing that game into my home. In my opinion, the rules are brutal. Every player has four colored pawns that travel around the board in an attempt to get "home." However, along the way, each player can send another's pawns back to Start, while issuing a very insincere "sorry." For some reason, it seems that a child's greatest joy from the game comes from bringing a sibling to tears. As a parent playing this game, you're faced with a moral dilemma. Do you change the rules along the way in order to keep peace around the table, or do you tough it out in an attempt to teach a valuable lesson about rule following to your children?

Have you ever had to "tough it out" in order to stick to your principles? It's important to establish rules in our personal lives, homes, and even places of work, but how do we begin? We need to inquire of the Lord.

Please read Numbers 27:1-11

The forty-year wandering in the wilderness was almost complete. The nation of Israel camped near the Jordan River, preparing themselves to enter the promised land. A census had been taken, counting the men of military age. Upon crossing the river and entering Canaan, each clan would receive an inheritance of the land based on the census numbers. Good plan. But there was one problem - Zelophehad had died without leaving any sons. There were five surviving daughters, but they were not counted in the census. The daughters approached Moses and pleaded their case.

According to verse 5, what did Moses do?

____

How did the Lord respond in verses 6-7?

____

Verse 8 begins with the word "Moreover." Briefly describe what happened in verses 8-11.

____

____

You go, daughters of Zelophehad! Such courage to approach Moses with this inquiry. How did they muster the confidence to do this? Let's sort through some important questions they must have answered as they prepared. Did they know who God was? Definitely. They had witnessed His presence and provision on a daily basis as they wandered in the wilderness. Did they know who they were? Yep. They were descendants of Joseph. *Joseph!* A man whose entire life demonstrated an unwavering faith in God and whose bones the Israelites carried with them to be buried in Canaan upon their arrival. Did the sisters understand their purpose? Most certainly. They were members of God's chosen people. With each death in the wilderness by those of the former generation, these young ladies would have been reminded to trust God and follow His leading. They were part of the generation God would use to change the world. OK, check, check, and check. Now to answer the question – "What Really Matters?" Well, without any brothers, they were the guardians of the family name. Land would soon be divided and their clan, as well as their father's name, would soon be forgotten. That mattered to them, it mattered to Moses, and it mattered to God.

What matters to you? In *The Deeper Life,* the question is posed: "What if someone were to come up and ask, 'Can you explain your values in two minutes or less?' Could you identify some uncompromising principles that are real for you and woven into the fabric of your daily existence? Are they so clear and dominant in your thinking that they are a framework for your daily life? Do you have a certain awareness that these principles spring from the Word of God?"

In order to become a woman of endurance, we need to know what matters. Then, we need to clearly communicate it. Our declared values must match our demonstrated values if we are to pursue lives of integrity.

When it comes to values there are two important factors. One is our declared values; the other involves our demonstrated values.

Declared values are what we say. Demonstrated values give evidence to what really matters by how we live. To avoid the dilemma of double-minded living and practical hypocrisy, we must come to a point where these two factors align.

> This idea can be stated as an equation:
> Declared + Demonstrated = Integrity
> Declared – Demonstrated = Hypocrisy

The task for us, if we are to live an integrated, meaningful life, is to come to a place of clarity and regular application so that our declared and demonstrated values are consistent and complimentary, not contradictory. A shallow, occasional engagement with the vital issue of values will not create a satisfying life. We must go deeper.

Making it Practical

Formulating your DECLARED values:
Write brief descriptions of the convictions you determine to be most important in your life. These are principles that you hope you would never compromise in the course of daily living.

____

____

____

____

____

____

____

Discovering your DEMONSTRATED values:
Here are some steps to assess your demonstrated values before you actually finalize the process by writing your values down:

- What dominates my thoughts? What do I really spend most of my time thinking about?
- Where do I spend my time? Time is life. If our time is spent on things that do not reflect our declared values, we have dissonance.
- How do I spend my money? Where your treasure is, there will your heart be also.
- How do I react? What do my reactions reveal about the values that motivate me?
- What would a brutally honest friend or associate say? Imagine their answers. Or, if you are really ready for some "reality," ask them. What demonstrated values do they see in your life that may be negative, destructive, or contradictory in comparison to your declared values?

In a spirit of humble dependence on God, review your *DECLARED VALUES* (in the first part of this exercise) and compare them to your *DEMONSTRATED VALUES* (in the second part) then seek His grace to deal with any contradictions you discover.

Organize to Memorize

Having thought deeply about your guiding principles, it may be worthwhile to organize them in an easy-to-remember form. Use this as a time to reaffirm your declared values that are supported by your demonstrated values and trust God for power to live accordingly.

Brenda's Values

B – Believe God has a plan (Jeremiah 29:11)
R – Remember His Word (Isaiah 66:2)
E – Encourage others in their walk (1 Thessalonian 5:11)
N – Nurture my family (2 Timothy 1:5)
D – Do my best (Hebrews 12:1-2)
A – Always give thanks (1 Corinthians 15:57-58)

Once this exercise is completed, you can record it in the Deeper Life Summary at the back of the book.

Go deeper by creating a "most admired" list and completing additional Values Discovery exercises in *The Deeper Life* book.

Group Discussion Questions

1. The daughters of Zelophehad had a choice to make. Should they follow the established rules or try to change them? Describe what you think they might have been feeling.
2. Have you ever had to a) enforce rules or b) change rules in order to stand up for your principles? How?
3. It has been said that we should cultivate in ourselves the qualities we most admire in others. Describe someone you admire. What key values have they demonstrated?

A Deeper Look at Priscilla

What Shall I Do?

My Priorities

Regardless of our stage in life, we never outgrow the need to stop and think; to consider our ways – and then to do things in the order of their importance.

— *Daniel Henderson*

Our journey is halfway over. We've traveled quite a distance through the pages of the Old Testament. Are you ready to check-in with some New Testament heroines? Today we'll begin our excursion in Corinth. Pack light. We won't be staying long.

Please read Acts 18:1-3, 18-21

Where did Paul first meet Aquila and Priscilla?

____

Where had they come from?

____

After spending time in Corinth in the home of Aquila and Priscilla, where did the threesome move to?

____

The name Priscilla means "worthy or venerable." Scholars believe that she may have belonged to a distinguished Roman family. Priscilla and her husband, Aquila, were Jews living in Rome during the reign of Claudius. After the Emperor expelled all Jews from Rome, the couple fled to Corinth. It was there that they met Paul.

Apparently, they all became friends quickly, because Paul stayed with them in their home for a year and a half. When Paul left Corinth, so did his new friends. Priscilla and Aquila traveled with Paul to Ephesus. Paul soon continued on his missionary journey, leaving Priscilla and Aquila in Ephesus.

What occurred in Acts 18:24-26?

____

____

With great humility, the couple invited the eloquent preacher Apollos back to their home to explain the Scriptures more accurately to him. Apollos' ministry and influence then grew exponentially. Because this couple made the spread of the Gospel a priority, they scattered seeds of influence wherever they went. Let's quickly follow the rest of their journey:

Read Romans 16:3-5. At some point, Priscilla and Aquila returned to Rome. How does Paul describe what they did for him in verse 4?

____

How were they using their home in Rome?

____

OK, so now they're home in Rome. Nice ring to it. Spaghetti every night for dinner, soothing music playing in the background . . . well maybe not, but at least Priscilla gets a chance to "nest" and hang a few pictures on her wall. But not for long.

Read 2 Timothy 4:19

At this point in their ministry, the couple had apparently returned to Ephesus. Paul was nearing his death and wanted to make sure that Timothy greeted his faithful friends and ministry partners. "Worthy" Priscilla had traveled from Rome to Corinth to Ephesus to Rome to Ephesus in her quest to share Christ and serve the Lord. She opened her home to strangers, welcomed believers on a regular basis for prayer and Bible study, then packed up and moved as the Lord directed. She was a woman who knew how to put "first things first" in order to live out her priorities. While this is the last mention of the couple in Scripture, tradition holds that Priscilla and Aquila ultimately laid down their lives for the sake of Christ. July 8th is the day set apart for them in Roman Martyrology. Her name (Prisca) appears often on monuments in Rome, and one of the oldest catacombs in the city – the Coemeterium Priscilla - was named in her honor.

As we seek to become a woman of endurance, we must be intentional about our priorities. God may not be asking us to set sail to a foreign country, but what is He asking us to do? Are we willing to take risks in order to fulfill our purpose in life? How often do we step outside our comfort zone in our desire to follow God?

Pondering our Priorities

Standing about 7,000 miles outside my comfort zone, I felt like I had stepped into a scene from a movie. My husband and I were in a dark hallway of an apartment building in Beijing waiting for clearance to join an illegal gathering. We had been given permission to visit a house church in China. In the three years we had been supporting the house church movement, over 2,500 new churches had been planted, resulting in 66,000 new believers. This was our opportunity to see with our own eyes what we had been reading about in reports. Our Chinese guide knocked, and then waited. Lights flashed and then he darted upstairs. We waited again. Finally, he motioned for us to hurry up two more flights. A door opened to a scene rarely witnessed by anyone outside of China. The small apartment was filled to capacity as the believers worshipped in secret. The sound of their singing filled the room. The young pastor greeted us warmly and welcomed us into the gathering. After the song came a prayer and then it was over. We were only allowed entrance in the final moments because our arrival might have been noticed by the authorities and dangerous to the congregation. Getting caught could mean being arrested or worse. This is the house church in China. It is secret. It is illegal. And it is exploding.

If attending church and reading the Bible were suddenly to be outlawed in your country, would you risk imprisonment in order to own a Bible or attend an illegal worship service? Thankfully, we are not faced with this decision in America. But it is a worthwhile exercise to stop and think about the priorities in our lives. What are we willing to sacrifice in order to put first things first? Noel Yeatts, humanitarian advocate and President of World Help, reminds women that "We each have a ticket to change the world. Some of us have time. Some of us have resources. Some have networks of influence. Others have great passion. But we each have a ticket. The question is, what will you do with yours?"[4]

A glance at the calendar of most women is enough to make us hyperventilate. We are over-committed and underappreciated. How do we begin to clean up the clutter in our lives in order to make room for things of eternal significance? We need to know when to say "no" and prioritize the commitments that deserve our "yes."

God has given us a theology, an identity, and a purpose for a reason: They help us identify the priorities that matter to Him. We need to strengthen our conviction to live for Him, even when other people may not understand our "no." Jesus said, "But seek first His kingdom and His righteousness; and all these things will be given to you as well." (Matthew 6:33)

Articulating Your Priorities

Use the chart on the next page to write down the specific commitments you will seek to pursue and protect on a daily basis. These are the "yeses" that will help you fulfill the Effective Purpose Statements you wrote out in the Purpose chapter. (See example)

---

4 Noel Brewer Yeatts, *Awake, Doing a World of Good One Person at a Time* (Grand Rapids: Baker Books, 2012), 150.

	Role *Mother*	Role *Wife*	Role *Small Group Leader*
Priority 1	Make prayer a priority in our home	Serve in ministry with my husband	Pray for the needs in our group

	Role	Role	Role
Priority 1			
Priority 2			
Priority 3			
Priority 4			

Once this exercise is completed, you can record it in the Deeper Life Summary at the back of the book.

Go deeper by reviewing priority guideposts and completing additional Priorities Discovery exercises in *The Deeper Life* book.

Group Discussion Questions

1. Read Matthew 6:19-21. What earthly treasures distract Christians from storing up treasures in heaven?
2. Priscilla lived a kingdom focused life outside her comfort zone. Have you ever stepped outside your comfort zone in order to pursue a heavenly treasure? Share with the group.
3. Describe a time when you had to say "no" in order to prioritize a "yes" commitment you made.

A Deeper Look at Lydia

What Shall I Do?

My Goals

A goal is a mark toward which you plan your life so that you can accomplish your priority commitments and live with integrity.

— *Daniel Henderson*

Welcome back. We survived our voyage and traveled quite a distance as we followed Priscilla on her journey. Are your feet tired yet? Maybe we can rest for a few moments by the riverbank. Water is so soothing and refreshing. Grab a bottle of it and let's get started.

Cleansing Water

The well dedication ceremony in the small Guatemalan village was interrupted just as the ribbon was about to be cut. A local village pastor asked to say a few words to our family. With hat in hand, he announced, "We've been waiting for this for many years, and now God has provided today. In the name of everybody here, we want to thank you." The grateful people of the village then applauded as my son cut the ribbon and the water began pouring out of the newly dug well. The tears in my eyes blurred my vision from seeing the smiling faces and laughing children as they played in the flowing water. A community of 2,500 people would now have access to clean water. No longer would they need to use the nearby river to bathe in or drink. What began as a dream – to travel as a family on a mission trip to Guatemala – turned into a goal – and then finally, a reality. Months of planning and saving and wondering if we could actually pull it off turned into joyous celebration. God had provided everything needed to fulfill His purpose and accomplish this goal. It was a dream come true.

Do you have a dream? In her book, "Love What You Do," Dana Spinola describes her own "dreaming sessions." She writes, "I start my dreaming sessions with a pretty simple prayer: 'God, please give me a curious mind to dream it and an open heart to believe it.'" Dana is founder and Chief Visionary Officer of fab'rik Boutiques. An accomplished entrepreneur, philanthropist, and mother of four, Dana is committed to reminding women to dream big and then chase those dreams relentlessly. Her success in the fashion industry began with a dream. Her dream turned into a plan. Priorities were made and goals were set. Was it easy? No, of course not. Along the way, God interrupted her plans. He nudged her in a new direction from time to time. She writes, "When God nudges you, or flat out calls you by name, he's holding out a gift . . . I could have ignored the nudge in my soul . . . but I didn't. Thank God."[5]

Interrupted Plans

On his second missionary journey, the Apostle Paul is prevented by the Holy Spirit from going where he and Silas intended to go. The reason? God needed to interrupt the plans of a particular woman in Philippi.

Please read Acts 16:6-15

Who did Paul meet by the river on the Sabbath?

____

What kind of business did Lydia of Thyatira engage in?

____

What did the Lord do for Lydia as she listened to Paul?

____

Paul's custom when entering a new town was to attend the local

5 "love what you do." Dana Spinola. p. 152-153

synagogue on the Sabbath. In order to form a synagogue, there must be at least 10 Jewish men. The fact that Paul went to the river on that first Sabbath indicates that there was no synagogue in town – not even 10 men who worshipped God. But there were women – and one woman in particular for whom God had a plan. Her name was Lydia.

Lydia was a businesswoman from Thyatira, a Macedonian colony known for its dyers. As a merchant of the expensive purple dye, Lydia would have been a very successful businesswoman. In addition to running a large household and profitable business, Lydia regularly attended ladies Bible study down by the river. Lydia was a woman with purpose, values, and priorities. With regard to her theology, we're told she was a worshiper of God. As for her identity, Lydia was likely of Greek descent, but it was evident that she was a Jewish proselyte seeking God.

So, imagine Lydia, the busy businesswoman, attending the regular ladies' prayer meeting by the river. It may have begun as a typical morning. Like most women, Lydia might have been keeping a running "to do" list in her head for the upcoming week. Then suddenly, Paul and his companions interrupt their ladies' group, as well as Lydia's demanding schedule. Since Paul was a Jewish preacher, the ladies would have invited him to speak. He spoke, her heart was opened to his message, and then Lydia and her household were quickly converted and baptized. Suddenly, her plans changed. She insisted that Paul and his companions stay at her house where a church was formed, and the gospel was introduced in Europe.

Did you catch that? A woman is the first recorded convert in Europe. She was a woman with plans. But she was willing to let God interrupt those plans. He held out a gift to Lydia. She accepted and became part of God's plan to spread the gospel throughout an entire continent.

Discovering God's Plan for Your Life

With a clear **theology** shaping our **identity** and motivating our **purposes**, we can begin to pursue a dream. Knowing our **values** and establishing our **priorities** sets us up for specific action. Now it's time to consecrate our hearts and minds to the Lord in order to set some **goals**. Six steps to creating good goals are outlined in *The Deeper Life*. We'll look at three of those steps to help get us started.

Use the guide below to help develop goals that will accomplish the priorities you identified in the previous chapter.

My Priority: (Choose one priority from the previous chapter)

Goals: (Write goals you need to accomplish in order to achieve this priority.)

1.
2.
3.

Review the following steps in developing goals. Are there any changes that you need to make?

Step One: Consecration

- What areas of my life will I have to surrender to God in order to accomplish these goals? (Review Proverbs 16:1–4)

Step Two: Preparation

- Are these goals specific? If not, write the specifics which ought to be clarified.
- Are these goals attainable? If not, adjust the ambition of the goal. If the hindrances can be overcome, how?

Step Three: Imagination

- What positive outcomes will occur if you achieve these goals? Write these down.
- What promises of God's word will you focus on to keep your faith growing? Write them down.
- When and how will I systematically pray about these targets?

Congratulations! You've begun a plan. Stay committed to your plan, but more importantly, stay committed to your God. If He interrupts, be flexible enough to trust Him for a better plan to accomplish His purposes.

Once this exercise is completed, you can record your goals in the Deeper Life Summary at the back of the book.

Go deeper by reviewing additional steps for creating goals and completing the Goals Discovery exercises in *The Deeper Life* book.

Group Discussion Questions

1. Describe a time when God interrupted your plans. How did the interruption change you?

2. Scripture doesn't tell us why Lydia was chosen to be Europe's first convert to Christianity. Why do you think she might have been picked out?

3. Has God given you a dream? Imagine that you've just received a large inheritance that allowed you to invest in that dream. Define 2 or 3 goals that will need to be executed in order to realize your dream.

A Deeper Look at the Samaritan Woman

When Shall I Do It?

My Time

I define time as my habitual expenditure of the stewardship of life.

— *Daniel Henderson*

Welcome back! I have a surprise for you. Today is a special day. The path we're following is going to lead us right through Samaria. *Samaria?* Before you pull out your GPS to research a better route, pause for just a moment. Look closely at the road ahead. Do you see that well? The Savior is going to show up there shortly. We don't want to miss a minute of this!

In the Nick of Time

As I looked at the clock on the evening of Thursday, May 11, 1989, I remember thinking, "Well, that's it. We're out of time." It was two days before my due date and three days before Mother's Day. Mother's Day was also Baby Dedication day in our church. A day where once a year parents had the opportunity to stand before the church, committing themselves to raising their child according to the Word of God.

Two years prior, I had given birth to my daughter four days before Mother's Day. We called the church and quickly arranged to be included in the dedication service. Naturally, when I learned that the due date for this baby was the day before Mother's Day, I knew – just knew – I would go into labor early and give birth in plenty of time to enjoy another dedication service with a newborn. I reminded the Lord of that goal EVERY DAY. Now, reflecting back on our goals worksheet, I realize that maybe it wasn't a consecrated goal, but don't try to con-

vince a hormonal pregnant woman of that incidental fact. My goal was about to evaporate and I became so irritated on that particular evening that I didn't notice the annoying Braxton Hicks contractions were occurring every five minutes. Eventually, the contractions caught my attention and the decision was made to go to the hospital. A few hours later, in the early morning hours of May 12th, a baby boy was placed in my arms. Two days later, we left the hospital in time to stop by church and dedicate two-day-old Nicholas. The hospital bracelet on my wrist in the photograph from that morning is a beautiful reminder of God's timing – and sense of humor. I've heard it said that God is never late, but He misses a few good opportunities to be early. The Bible says it another way – "in the fullness of time."

Please read John 4:1-42

Where did this scene take place? (v. 5)

____

What did Jesus ask the woman for in verse 7?

____

What did He offer her in verse 10?

____

What request did He make of her in verse 16?

____

What did he reveal to her in verse 26?

____

When was the last time you experienced an extraordinary moment in the midst of a very ordinary day? When God interrupts your life, He is inviting you into a *kairos* moment with Him. *Kairos* is the idea of a fixed moment or season of opportunity. This is the experience of our life when time stands still and something truly "timeless" happens. It is unique from *chronos*, from which we get the word "chronology." *Chronos* is the clock that pushes us to the next appointment and runs out before we have finished with our daily responsibilities. Both of these words indicate time. The difference between these two words is the difference between a minute and a moment. We have not understood the value of time until we firmly grasp, actively anticipate, and purposefully pursue the moments God places before us.

Consider Your *Chronos*

Let's take a minute to consider the moments of our ordinary days. Are we anticipating the extraordinary opportunities that can occur? Could it be that our schedules are so full that we don't even notice the One sitting by the well waiting to refresh us with Living Water? Reflect for a moment on Jesus' words to the Samaritan woman:

> *Yet a time is coming and has now come when the true worshipers will worship the Father in the Spirit and in truth, for they are the kind of worshipers the Father seeks.*
>
> John 4:23

The *time* is coming and has *now* come. If you desire to be the kind of worshiper the Father seeks, then the time has now come. The Father is seeking those who will worship in spirit and truth. When we set aside time to worship the Lord, it is never wasted time. *The Living Bible* paraphrases Proverbs 10:27 this way: "Reverence for God adds hours to each day."

Finding *Kairos* in the Chaos of *Chronos*

We can never predict the timing of a *kairos* moment – we can't post it on our refrigerator or set an appointment on our phone. But when it occurs, we need to stop everything because it's God's way of telling us it's time for a divine appointment.

John 4:4 tells us that. Oh, what beautiful words. Jesus *had* to go. According to God's sovereign clock, it was time. Why was it necessary to meet this woman at this moment in this town? Because it was time to shatter a few barriers – of a man speaking to a woman in public; of a rabbi speaking to an outcast; of a Jew willing to interact with a Samaritan. In addition, it was time to reveal Jesus as Messiah to this woman by this well in this town. Finally, it was time to gather a harvest of souls for the Kingdom. On an ordinary day, performing an ordinary task, this ordinary woman experienced an extraordinary encounter. It was a *kairos* moment. She would begin her journey to a deeper life as she discussed her theology and identity with her Creator. During the course of their conversation, Jesus revealed Himself, confronted her sin and fulfilled His purpose in her life.

One of the most important elements in *kairos* living is remembering to be open to the people who enter into your daily life. Wise time-management includes being available to the spontaneous work of the Holy Spirit. In short, make the most of your time.

In Appendix 2, you'll find a sample of my prayer journal. It helps me to devote time each day in worship-based prayer, and then align my schedule to accomplish my priorities and look for *kairos* in the chaos of my *chronos*.

Record some of your thoughts with regard to time:

____

____

____

Once this exercise is completed, you can record a "Time" statement in the Deeper Life Summary at the back of the book.

Go deeper by evaluating your schedule and completing Time Discovery exercises in *The Deeper Life* book.

Group Discussion Questions

1. Describe a recent *kairos* moment when something extraordinary happened in the midst of an ordinary day.
2. Think back to the story of Hagar. Do you notice any similarities in her story to the story of the Samaritan woman?
3. How can you more consistently and consciously acknowledge the presence of God in the minutes of your day?

A Deeper Look at Eunice

How Will I Finish?

My Legacy

In the end, a deeper life must be a life deposited into the fertile soil of eternal souls through the transforming seeds of truth.

— *Daniel Henderson*

We've made it to our final stop on our deeper life journey. Along the way, we have answered several questions – *Who is God, Who am I, Why am I Here, What Really Matters, What Shall I Do, How Shall I do It,* and *When Shall I do It?* You have invested much time in this journey. Rest assured, it has been an investment of eternal significance.

Becoming a Legacy Leaver

My friend Jill lived a deep, meaningful life with purpose. She knew her God and embraced her identity in Him. As a professor at a large Christian university, Jill invested time in things that mattered to her – her family, her students, and her friends.

Time spent with Jill never involved superficial chatting. She always desired to go deeper in conversations. On one occasion, as several of us gathered for lunch, Jill posed the question, "Which woman in the Bible do you most admire?" She then proceeded to go around the table, allowing each woman to share her answer. Of course, there are many heroines in Scripture. It was difficult for everyone to choose. When it was my turn to reveal my most-admired woman, I simply said "Eunice." For a moment I enjoyed the confused looks around the table. Then I explained. "Eunice is named in Scripture because of the influence she had on her son, Timothy. Eunice was a legacy leaver." Since we were all moms around the table, it sparked an interesting discussion.

Ultimately, when all is said and done, what matters most is the impact our lives had on others.

Not long after that luncheon, Jill was killed, along with her teenage son, by a drunk driver. The thousands who attended her funeral were a testament to the legacy of this incredible woman and the impact she left on those she touched. Dr. Jill Jones was a legacy leaver.

Ladies, we need to begin thinking today about our legacy. How do you want to be remembered? What will your impact be?

Please read 2 Timothy 1:1-5

To whom was this letter written?

___

What was Paul reminded of when he wrote this letter?

___

From whom did Timothy learn about faith?

___

Eunice was the daughter of Lois and mother of Timothy. She was a Jewess who married a Greek man. We are not told her husband's name, and the implication is that he was not a worshiper of God. It is assumed that Eunice was a widow when Paul first visited their city.

Please read Acts 16:1-5

Why did Paul want Timothy to join them?

___

Timothy was a young man – most likely in his teens or early twenties. It is believed that Paul led Timothy to Christ on his first missionary journey to Lystra (Acts 14:6-23). During Paul's second missionary journey, Timothy was asked to join Paul and Silas. Young Timothy would be mentored by Paul and remain friends of the Apostle for the rest of Paul's life. He is frequently mentioned in Paul's epistles and served as Paul's representative on many occasions. Timothy also served as pastor of the church at Ephesus. His impact on the world and the Church will not be fully known until eternity.

As Paul wrote his final letter to his dear friend and protégé, it is worth noting that Timothy's legacy would forever be linked to the faithful teaching of his mother and grandmother.

Please read 2 Timothy 3:14-15

When did Timothy first begin learning the Scriptures?

Oh, how I love Eunice. Now that I'm a grandmother, I also have a deep admiration for Lois. Although they are only briefly mentioned in Scripture, we can glean enough to know that life was not easy for this dynamic duo. Eunice, a Jewish woman, married a Greek man, a Gentile. The ramifications of that were two-fold. First, she would have been considered a traitor to her faith, and secondly, her son, Timothy, would have been viewed as a Gentile since his father was Greek. But these women would not be deterred from passing down a spiritual heritage – teaching young Timothy the Holy Scriptures from childhood. Their legacy of faith would prepare Timothy for a life that surely surpassed all they could have asked or imagined for this young man.

In her book, "The Resolution for Women," Priscilla Shirer addresses this issue of legacy. She writes, "We have each been called to leave a godly legacy, to pass the baton of His grace and truth to others, who will then take it to lengths and destinations we will never go ourselves. This is not an option. This is a heavenly mandate."[6]

Passing the Baton

In the 2016 Summer Olympics the United States women were favored to win the 4 x 100 relay. But during the second heat, Allyson Felix was bumped by the runner in the next lane, causing her to

6 Priscilla Shirer, The Resolution for Women (Nashville: B&H, 2011), 257.

drop the baton in the handoff. Her teammate, English Gardner, later described those tense moments. She said that Allyson, who is normally a very composed runner, was frantic and in agony over the incident. But then, suddenly, she said, Allyson became still and calmly said, "pick up the baton and run."[7]

As I watched those events unfold, I realized that when we speak of legacy, we often focus on passing the baton. But life seldom allows us the opportunity to give a perfect handoff. People encroach in our lane. We get bumped. Sometimes we get so off balance that we drop the baton. We have a choice in that moment. We can agonize over our mistakes. Or, if we can just be still, we might hear the voice of the Lord saying, "pick up the baton and run." The ladies were given another opportunity to run the race and they won the Gold Medal.

The Deeper Life encourages us to reflect on the truth that only imperfect people leave a legacy. "A legacy is not about some standard of unachievable virtue. . . . Rather, the inspiration of a legacy is composed of difficulties endured, mistakes made right, lessons learned through pain, and tough relationships graced by the power of forgiveness and reconciliation."

The ultimate goal of our legacy is the "Well done!" commendation of Christ in eternity. The earthly benefit of a legacy is that we inspired those who knew us to embrace the same values and continue running the race.

The World Needs Your Legacy

So, what can you leave as a visible reminder of your legacy? Consider writing an "end of life" letter. Imagine it is the last hour of your life. Address the letter to the most important people of your journey. As you write, consider these themes: What do I want others to remember about me? What opportunities and risks have enriched my life? What has God's blessing looked like during my journey? What regrets must I surrender and trust to the mercy of God? Be

7 English Gardner, NBC Today, August 20. 2016.

as honest and specific as possible. After you finish the letter, ask yourself: "What do I need to focus on every day in order for this letter to be an authentic representation of my legacy?"

The world needs your legacy. Now, pick up your baton and go run.

Be sure to record your thoughts on Legacy in the Deeper Life Summary at the back of the book.

Go deeper by clarifying the kind of legacy you want to leave and completing additional Legacy Discovery exercises in *The Deeper Life* book.

Group Discussion Questions

1. Do you know someone (maybe you!) who picked up a dropped baton and continued running their race? Share the story without embarrassing the individual.
2. Describe someone you know with Eunice qualities – a legacy leaver who pours into others.
3. Explain how your theology, identity, purpose, values, priorities, goals and time help ensure the legacy that you want to leave.

Epilogue

"I am the Lord's servant," Mary answered. "May it be to me as you have said." Then the angel left her.

— Luke 1:38

Every journey eventually comes to an end. Do you dread packing up after a wonderful trip? I do. For some reason, things don't seem to fit in the suitcase quite the same. Maybe it's the souvenirs I've picked up along the way. They get tucked in here and there and will eventually become special keepsakes after I'm home.

Can we squeeze in one more memento before we say good-bye? It doesn't seem right to end this adventure together without stopping by Elizabeth's house. Her young relative, Mary, is visiting.

Luke describes the visit of these two women. After the announcement by the angel Gabriel to Mary that she would give birth to the Son of God, the young woman hurried to the home of Elizabeth. There were many differences in the two women – one was old, one young. One had been married many years. The other, newly engaged. They did, however, share one extraordinary similarity. Both women were highly favored by their heavenly Father. They were the chosen mothers of two boys who would grow up and change the world. It's understandable that young Mary needed this special time with her older relative. Can you imagine their conversations? With every glance at Zechariah, who also encountered Gabriel, Mary would have been assured that the angel's pronouncement would come true at the proper time. (Luke 1:19-20).

We don't know if Elizabeth lived long enough to see her son fulfill God's purpose for his life. We do know that she was filled with joy at John's birth (Luke 1:57-79).

As for Mary, the biblical account allows us to drop in on her as a young mom (Luke 2:7-39; Matthew 2:11-25), then again as a mother in the throes of raising a family (Luke 2:48), and then later as the mother of an adult son (John 2:5), and finally as a worshiper of her Son as her Risen Savior (Acts 1:14). What a life of transformation!

Imagine having the opportunity to interview Mary in her latter years. First, I would ask her about all the things she treasured and pondered in her heart (Luke 2:19). Of course, I would want to hear stories of Jesus' childhood and all that she witnessed as He grew in wisdom and stature and favor with God and men. But before we conclude our conversation, I would ask Mary to reflect on her answers to the questions we've been asking ourselves:

1. **Who is God?**
2. **Who am I?**
3. **Why am I Here?**
4. **What Really Matters?**
5. **What Shall I do?**
6. **How Shall I do it?**
7. **When Shall I do it?**
8. **How Will I Finish?**

Mary learned the secret to living a deeper life. It began with a life dedicated to knowing and serving God. She recognized her identity in Him and understood her purpose. Mary lived out her values, established her priorities, and fulfilled every goal the Lord placed on her heart. She embraced each God-ordained moment and left a legacy of humble endurance.

As we give Mary a hug good-bye, take a glance over your shoulder and look how far we traveled. We have traversed through the pages of Scripture, covering several millennia. With each stop, we've learned a secret or two to living a deeper life. That tiny movement back there on the horizon might be Grandma Eve. She's watching you run your race and cheering you on. This is your moment to carry the baton. Don't stop until you've given a good hand-off. The next generation is counting on you. Your footsteps will help guide the way for others to live a deeper life.

Appendix 1

Our Essential Identity

Essential identity reflects *Who I am* in light of the person and work of Jesus Christ. Spiritual birth delivers us from darkness into light and makes us new people. "If anyone is in Christ, he is a new creature; the old things pass away; behold, new things have come." 2 Corinthians 5:17 (NASB)

How to Be Born Again

Mankind is made in the spiritual image of God, to be like Him in character. We are the supreme object of God's creation. Although we have tremendous potential for good, we are marred by an attitude of disobedience toward God called sin. This attitude separates us from God. Genesis 1:27; Psalm 8:3-6; Isaiah 53:6a; Romans 3:23; Isaiah 59:1-2

Salvation is a gift from God to mankind. We can never make up for our sin by self-improvement or good works. Only by trusting in Jesus Christ as God's offer of forgiveness can we be saved from sin's penalty. Eternal life begins the moment one receives Jesus Christ into one's life by faith. Romans 6:23; Ephesians 2:8-9; John 14:6, 1:12; Titus 3:5; Galatians 3:26; Romans 5:1

To receive this free gift of salvation, you need to A) Admit that you are a sinner; B) Believe that Jesus died for your sins and rose again; and C) Confess that Jesus is Lord. If you are ready to receive Jesus as your Savior, you can pray a prayer like this:

> *God, I admit that I have sinned against you. I am sorry for the sin in my life. Please forgive me. I am trusting*

> *Jesus to be my Savior. I believe in Him and confess Him as my Lord. Jesus, please come into my life and help me to live for You. Amen.*

To make a decision to receive Jesus as Lord is the most important decision you will ever make. If you have prayed this prayer, you are now born again. Welcome to the family!

Appendix 2

Prayer Journal Pages

Wise time management includes the decision to capture moments for personal renewal. Jesus understood the necessity of spending time in the Father's presence. In Matthew 6:9-13, He gave us a pattern for praying which includes Reverence, Response, Requests, and Readiness. To learn more about this prayer pattern, read *Transforming Prayer, How Everything Changes When You Seek God's Face,* by Daniel Henderson.

Reverence ♥ God You are . . . (upward) ↑

Response ♥ Lord, I surrender . . . (downward) ↓

Requests ♥ Lord I need . . . (inward) ←

Readiness ♥ Lord, I trust You to . . . (outward) →

Today's Date

Finding *Kairos* in the chaos of my *Chronos*

Today's Schedule

Today's Priorities

Kairos Moments that occurred today:

1. ______________________________

2. ______________________________

3. ______________________________

YOUR DEEPER LIFE SUMMARY

After completing the exercises at the end of each chapter, you can record your written statements here.

- The **FOUNDATION** section will help you affirm your theology, identity, purposes and values.
- The **IMPLEMENTATION** section will enable you to identify key priorities, establish goals to accomplish those priorities, and manage your time to achieve the goals.
- The **DESTINATION** section will inspire you to continue toward the ultimate longing to leave a legacy that really matters.

FOUNDATION

Who is God? (My Theology)

My God is . . .

Who am I? (My Identity)

My Essential Identity:

I, ______________________________ (name) am . . .

Why am I here? (My Purpose)

My eternal purpose is . . .

My earthly purpose is . . .

My explicit purposes

As a ______________ (role), my purpose is . . .

As a ______________ (role), my purpose is . . .

As a ______________ (role), my purpose is . . .

As a ______________ (role), my purpose is . . .

As a ______________ (role), my purpose is . . .

What Really Matters? (My Values)

My life values are . . .

IMPLEMENTATION:

What Should I Do? (My Priorities) → How Should I Do It? (My Goals)

Role: ____________________

PRIORITIES	GOALS
1.	1a.
	1b.
2.	2a.
	2b.

3.	3a.
	3b.

Role: ____________________________

PRIORITIES	GOALS
1.	1a.
	1b.
2.	2a.
	2b.
3.	3a.
	3b.

Role: ____________________________

PRIORITIES	GOALS
1.	1a.
	1b.
2.	2a.
	2b.

3. 3a.

3b.

When Should I Do It? (My Time)

How I will find *"kairos"* in the chaos of my *"chronos"* to accomplish my goals . . .

DESTINATION

How Will I Finish? (My Legacy)

What I want others to remember about me is . . .

Tips for leading The Deeper Life of Women in the Bible

Studying God's Word together always impacts our lives in powerful and sometimes unpredictable ways. If you are preparing to lead a small group study of *The Deeper Life of Women in the Bible*, here are a few guidelines to help you prepare.

If possible, schedule ten weeks to complete this study. On week one, read through the introduction together, then dig deep into the discussion questions. Weeks two through nine will focus on the eight enduring women and their corresponding deeper life principle. Week ten should be used to recap the eight principles. Discuss the Epilogue and review your small group's Deeper Life Summaries (pp. 70-75). The following tips will help you plan for a typical 90-minute group meeting:

1. Read. Prior to the session, participants should read the assigned chapter from *The Deeper Life of Women in the Bible*. This study is designed to supplement the book, *The Deeper Life, Satisfying the Eight Vital Longings of the Soul*. You will want to have a copy of this book and read the corresponding chapter as your group members may refer to it.

2. Remember to begin with prayer. If you're like me, your mind is working overtime with details to dive into and points you've pondered. Remember Who is truly leading this discussion and drawing women closer to Him. Invite Christ into your discussion – to lead, to teach, and to transform hearts and minds.

3. Reflect. Briefly review the Deeper Life Question and Issue this week is seeking to address.

4. Recap. Summarize the story of the biblical deeper life woman and invite ladies to share their answers to the questions within the assigned chapter.

5. Relate. Each chapter includes three discussion questions to help spark meaningful conversation. Here are some guidelines for leading the conversation:

- This is a discussion, not a lecture. Resist the temptation to do all the talking, and to answer the questions yourself. Don't be afraid of a few moments of silence while women formulate their answers.
- Encourage everyone to participate. Don't let one person dominate, but also don't pressure quieter members to speak during the first couple of sessions. After one person answers, don't immediately move on; ask what other women think or say, "Would someone who hasn't shared like to add anything?"
- Affirm all answers with a "thanks" or "great answer." If an answer is clearly wrong, ask "What led you to that conclusion?" or ask what the rest of the group thinks. If a disagreement arises, don't feel like you need to immediately shut down the discussion! The discussion can draw out important perspectives, and if you can't resolve it there, offer to research it further and return to the issues next week.
- Detour when necessary. If an important question is raised that is not in the study guide, take time to discuss it. If you have already covered a written question previously, skip it. Allow the Holy Spirit room to maneuver and follow His prompting when the discussion changes direction.

6. Renew your mind. As you close in prayer, choose a Scripture verse to help guide your prayer time. Begin your prayer with worship by acknowledging the worthiness of God. As you transition into your requests, invite the ladies to pray aloud in sentence prayers. Remember, God is worthy, and we are needy. Keep renewing your mind in the worthiness of God to address every need of the women in your group. If time is limited, bring notecards and invite women to write out their prayer requests and exchange cards. Include a cell phone number on the card so that encouraging text messages can be sent throughout the week.

More DEEPER LIFE resources

Plenty of books talk about living a deeper life. This one shows you how -- how to truly discover the answers to life's core questions and live them out in your thoughts, words, and actions. **The Deeper Life, Satisfying the 8 Vital Longings of Your Soul** shares the principles and practices that are vital to a transformed life. It explains the longings that resonate in our souls – longings such as wanting to know God more fully, to know ourselves better, and to spend our time on things that matter.

21 Days to a Deeper Life includes 21 daily readings along with application questions and an audio prayer to follow along with each day.

Interested in going even deeper? Work with a trained Deeper Life coach to help you realize the full potential of this renewal process and the application of the vital answers to your deepest longings. To inquire about personal Deeper Life coaching, contact Brenda@8QCoaching.com.

Praying People supporting **Praying Pastors** leading **Praying Churches** for **Supernatural Gospel Impact.**